WE NEED TREES!

CARING FOR OUR PLANET

I0879630

By VITA JIMÉNEZ
Illustrations by GEORGE ERMOS
Music by ERIK KOSKINEN

CANTATA
LEARNING

WWW.CANTATALEARNING.COM

CANTATA
LEARNING

Published by Cantata Learning
1710 Roe Crest Drive
North Mankato, MN 56003
www.cantatalearning.com

Copyright © 2018 Cantata Learning

All rights reserved. No part of this publication may be reproduced
in any form without written permission from the publisher.

A note to educators and librarians from the publisher: Cantata Learning has provided the following data to assist in book processing and suggested use of Cantata Learning product.

Publisher's Cataloging-in-Publication Data
Prepared by Librarian Consultant: Ann-Marie Begnaud
Library of Congress Control Number: 2016938068
We Need Trees : Caring for Our Planet
Series: Me, My Friends, My Community : Caring for Our Planet
By Vita Jiménez
Illustrations by George Ermos
Music by Erik Koskinen
Summary: In this catchy song paired with colorful illustrations, children learn the reasons we need trees.
ISBN: 978-1-63290-781-3 (library binding/CD)
ISBN: 978-1-68410-107-8 (paperback)
Suggested Dewey and Subject Headings:
Dewey: E 582.16
LCSH Subject Headings: Trees – Juvenile literature. | Environmental responsibility – Juvenile literature. | Trees – Songs and music – Texts. | Environmental responsibility – Songs and music – Texts. | Trees – Juvenile sound recordings. | Environmental responsibility – Juvenile sound recordings.
Sears Subject Headings: Trees. | Environmental protection. | School songbooks. | Children's songs. | Folk music – United States.
BISAC Subject Headings: JUVENILE NONFICTION / Science & Nature / Trees & Forests. | JUVENILE NONFICTION / Music / Songbooks. | JUVENILE NONFICTION / Science & Nature / Environmental Conservation & Protection.

Book design and art direction: Tim Palin Creative
Editorial direction: Flat Sole Studio
Music direction: Elizabeth Draper
Music written and produced by Erik Koskinen and recorded at Real Phonic Studios

Printed in the United States of America in North Mankato, Minnesota.
072017 0367CGF17

ACCESS THE MUSIC!
SCAN CODE WITH MOBILE APP
CANTATALEARNING.COM

TIPS TO SUPPORT LITERACY AT HOME

WHY READING AND SINGING WITH YOUR CHILD IS SO IMPORTANT

Daily reading with your child leads to increased academic achievement. Music and songs, specifically rhyming songs, are a fun and easy way to build early literacy and language development. Music skills correlate significantly with both phonological awareness and reading development. Singing helps build vocabulary and speech development. And reading and appreciating music together is a wonderful way to strengthen your relationship.

READ AND SING EVERY DAY!

TIPS FOR USING CANTATA LEARNING BOOKS AND SONGS DURING YOUR DAILY STORY TIME

1. As you sing and read, point out the different words on the page that rhyme. Suggest other words that rhyme.
2. Memorize simple rhymes such as Itsy Bitsy Spider and sing them together. This encourages comprehension skills and early literacy skills.
3. Use the questions in the back of each book to guide your singing and storytelling.
4. Read the included sheet music with your child while you listen to the song. How do the music notes correlate to the words of the song?
5. Sing along on the go and at home. Access music by scanning the QR code on each Cantata book. You can also stream or download the music for free to your computer, smartphone, or mobile device.

Devoting time to daily reading shows that you are available for your child. Together, you are building language, literacy, and listening skills.

Have fun reading and singing!

Trees are an important **natural resource**. They give us **oxygen** and shade. They provide food and homes for animals. We also use the wood from trees to make homes, furniture, paper, and many other things.

To learn why we need trees, turn the page and sing along!

Why are trees important?

We need trees for the clean air we **breathe**.
We need trees for the shade of their leaves.

We need trees for wood, paper, and homes.
We need trees for fruits and nuts to grow.

We need trees.
We need trees!

Trees help keep air cool and clean.
They give us oxygen to breathe.

For clean air, we need trees.

For clean air, we need trees.

Trees are homes for birds and bees.

Many animals nest in trees.

For animal homes, we need trees.

For animal homes, we need trees.

We need trees for the clean air we breathe.
We need trees for the shade of their leaves.

We need trees for wood, paper, and homes.
We need trees for fruits and nuts to grow.

We need trees.
We need trees!

Trees grow nuts and fruits to eat:
apples, almonds, and other treats.

For many foods, we need trees.
For many foods, we need trees.

For each tree that is cut down,
plant a new one in the ground.

We need forests, so plant new trees.

We need forests, so plant new trees.

On Arbor Day we **celebrate**
all the ways that trees are great.

We celebrate the ways we need trees!

We celebrate. We need trees!

We celebrate. Trees are great!

We clap and cheer. We need trees!

We need trees for the clean air we breathe.
We need trees for the shade of their leaves.

We need trees for wood, paper, and homes.
We need trees for fruits and nuts to grow.

We need trees.

We need trees!

SONG LYRICS

We Need Trees

We need trees for the clean air we breathe.
We need trees for the shade of their leaves.
We need trees for wood, paper, and homes.
We need trees for fruits and nuts to grow.
We need trees.
We need trees!

Trees help keep air cool and clean.
They give us oxygen to breathe.
For clean air, we need trees.
For clean air, we need trees.

Trees are homes for birds and bees.
Many animals nest in trees.
For animal homes, we need trees.
For animal homes, we need trees.

We need trees for the clean air we breathe.
We need trees for the shade of their leaves.
We need trees for wood, paper, and homes.
We need trees for fruits and nuts to grow.
We need trees.
We need trees!

Trees grow nuts and fruits to eat:
apples, almonds, and other treats.
For many foods, we need trees.
For many foods, we need trees.

For each tree that is cut down,
plant a new one in the ground.
We need forests, so plant new trees.
We need forests, so plant new trees.

On Arbor Day we celebrate
all the ways that trees are great.
We celebrate the ways we need trees!
We celebrate. We need trees!
We celebrate. Trees are great!
We clap and cheer. We need trees!

We need trees for the clean air we breathe.
We need trees for the shade of their leaves.
We need trees for wood, paper, and homes.
We need trees for fruits and nuts to grow.
We need trees.
We need trees!

We Need Trees

Americana
Erik Koskinen

Chorus

Verse 3
Trees grow nuts and fruits to eat:
apples, almonds, and other treats.
For many foods, we need trees.
For many foods, we need trees.

Verse 4
For each tree that is cut down,
plant a new one in the ground.
We need forests, so plant new trees.
We need forests, so plant new trees.

Chorus

ACCESS THE MUSIC!
SCAN CODE WITH MOBILE APP
CANTATALEARNING.COM

GLOSSARY

breathe—to take air in and then let it out

celebrate—to do something special

natural resource—something found in nature, such as trees, that people use

oxygen—a gas in the air that people need to breathe

plant—to place something, such as a seed or young tree, in the ground so it can grow

GUIDED READING ACTIVITIES

1. The title of this book is *We Need Trees!* Do you think that it is a good title? Why or why not?

2. Look around your home or classroom. List all of the things you find that are made of wood.

3. There are many kinds of trees. What type of trees grow near you? Draw one of the trees near where you live.

TO LEARN MORE

Lepetit, Angie. *Three Cheers for Trees!* North Mankato, MN: Capstone, 2013.

Rissman, Rebecca. *Arbor Day*. Chicago: Heinemann, 2010.

Rustad, Martha. *What's in a Tree?* North Mankato, MN: Capstone, 2016.

Veitch, Catherine. *Learning about Trees*. Chicago: Raintree, 2014.